SHAKING

THE

PERSIMMON

TREE

SHAKING THE PERSIMMON TREE

MARC WOODWARD

Sea Crow Press

Sea Crow Press

Shaking the Persimmon Tree

Copyright © 2022 by Marc Woodward

First Edition Trade Paperback

Trade Paperback ISBN: 979-8-9850080-0-5

Ebook ISBN: 979-8-9850080-5-0

Cover Image Painted by Jesse Woodward, www.JesseWoodwardart.com

Cover Design by PopKitty Design

Interior Formatting by Mary Petiet

www.seacrowpress.com

BY MARC WOODWARD

The Tin Lodes (with Andy Brown)

Hide Songs

A Fright of Jays

ACKNOWLEDGMENTS

My thanks to the editors of the following magazines and journals in which a number of these poems appeared: Acumen Literary Journal, Aesthetica Magazine, The Blue Nib, Clear Poetry, Dreich, Ofi, Open Arts Forum, Otter, Poetry Salzburg Review, Prole Magazine, Riggwelter, Riptide Journal, The Sunday Tribune, The West Review. Inheritance previously appeared in my chapbook *A Fright of Jays* published by Maquette Press.

My thanks to my good friend Andy Brown for his mentoring and advice, and as always to my wonderful wife Sarah for her support and love. And to my children, Tom, Jack, and Olivia, for all the joy and laughter.

My thanks also to Mary Petiet and her team at Sea Crow Press, I'm delighted to join their roster of authors.

Thanks too to the village of Serramonacesca, Abruzzo, where a number of these poems started life, and of course, to the inspiring hills and weather of Devon.

Finally a nod to all those living with Parkinson's Disease, young and old. Stay strong.

CONTENTS

Dedicated to my parents Judy & Mervyn

Thin Luigi stands next to me and points
at the sun's red arc settling on the ridge,
clocking out of its daily labour
in the hot factory of summer.
He says that in the long days of June
it sets further towards the Gran Sasso
then, as each day passes, creeps its way
south along the far Morrone ridge.
But today is Ferragosto and the sun
still has much travelling to do.
For now I'm glad its hot eye is closing
on another sweltering afternoon.
I offer Luigi a beer which he declines,
as usual, and in my poor Italian
try to say how a calendar could be made
by putting markers on the hills
according to the setting sun.
He smiles, nods and speaks again.
I smile and nod too, feeling sure
neither of us have understood a word.
We watch the quick descent of the sun
the top edge just showing now...
                    ...and now gone.
The bee-eaters are still chirruping,
but in the trees the last golden orioles
have calmed their fluting song.
Thin Luigi sighs and says *Ciao Marco,
ci vediamo*... and wanders off up the lane.
His dogs are barking in their pen.
I shake a mosquito from my ankle
then look back at the dark mountain ridge
and the house lights coming on in Serra.

If I were constant like Thin Luigi,
I could observe all the sunsets I'd need
to mark down and make that calendar
then use it to count the fallow days
which fall between you and me
each one like a flake of snow settling
on the slopes of Monte Amaro.

THE JEWELLED BEETLES

Sweeping out the shut-up house
I found them on the bedroom floor:
the jewelled beetles. Purple and green.
In June they must have hatched in there
and grown enough on dust and air
to earn their sheen, their brilliancy.
Wanderers on arid marble,
like survivors of a chrome plane
downed in a desert, seeking water.
Beyond the glass the laurel waved;
bamboo canes inched ever skyward.

On my palm their carapaces
lay vibrant and glowing - and dead.
Like that vintage scarab bracelet
I bought for you when we were kids.
Were those bright beetles the real thing
- preserved in their filigree mounts -
or some costume jewellery mock up?
I placed *my* beetles in a ring,
snapped and tagged you on Instagram
- then tossed their sad husks to the wind
and turned back to the dusty room.

The Boar

Beyond the garden boundary
past the halo of the terrace lights,
the undergrowth is shaking
to the soft grunts of a cinghiale.
I can't see him but I know he's there.

Along the night-sweat lane
near the house with the rusted vines
big white dogs are sounding off,
barking their ignorance
into the night, over and over.

I could walk out in the grass
to the edge of the rustling dark,
sure the boar would batter away
wary of my man-stink
and the shotgun I might carry.

But we play this stand off,
me here, the boar in the bushes,
for we each know our place
and no good thing can come
from forcing a meeting.

And what if it isn't a boar
rattling unseen in the canes?
Perhaps it's something else
pulling down the green leaves,
tearing up the teeming soil?

So I stay by the moth-speckled lights
for fear of unknowable things -
not the bristly pig in the bush
with his pinhole eyes, rooty tusks,
stupidly dainty on cloven heels.

That shape though: the bulk of a boar,
of a high and hump-backed hill,
of a stoop-shouldered sky,
awful in its absence and presence -
that shape is waiting for me,

aware one day I'll have no choice
but to push into the shadows
and find the beast shaking
at a persimmon tree
knowing the fruit must surely fall.

THE THREAD

Standing on a strand made velvet
by the shadow of the headland,
she arcs a great beach pole and casts,
hurling the hook, line and lead weight

far, far out beyond the breakers
to the seam where ocean and sky
are stitched lazily together
and there the sinker drops to plumb

ancient, amniotic water.
She snags the weave of the seabed,
begins the process of reeling
and as she does the rusty sand

beneath her feet begins to shift -
she's sinking in with every turn,
every wind, yet cannot stop
the spooling as she disappears

into the sand with the sand fleas,
down through the dark ammonite lodes,
as if the hook had caught her heel
and still she reels and reels and reels,

until she's gone with the sea and
the land and the great cloudy sky
following down into this hole
of her own persistence, like all

of it, every fish, bird, mammal,
was attached to the one same thread
she'd been pulling since she was born,
like all our generations dead,

careless for the unravelling.

ON SITTING WITH A RETIRED PILOT WATCHING FOR WATER VOLES

Motionless on camping chairs
we listen for little splashes
from the ditch at the marsh's edge.

I've released sixty-five of them.
They'll take all weekend to burrow in.
If the foxes don't find them first...

The day hangs limply. The stubborn sky
looks like it could go either way.
On the river a blue dinghy dithers.

A little <plop!> ten yards upstream.
There!
            The bullrushes quiver and rasp.
A blackbird lands on the cut grass

then takes off again.
                        If it works
I'll feel I've given something back.
    An offset of water voles.

I'd heard some time ago it had gone
to his bones. He'd far exceeded
the doctors' grim expectations.

I love days like this when it's so still
you feel it could last forever.
When I was flying I'd have worried

about thunder. On a day like this.
Now I don't care. I think maybe
I'd welcome it.

Listen...

There

LEAVING SWITZERLAND

The train emerged from the fist of the Alps
to trundle across the alluvial floor.

Melt-water hurtled through granite boulders,
garden fires died under their own tall ghosts.

A helicopter chewed the widening sky,
the light as clean as a surgical saw.

> *Going the other way the week before*
> *he'd held her hand the entire journey*
>
> *worrying that she'd not be strong enough*
> *to undergo the strain of travelling,*
>
> *the sideways stares of other passengers,*
> *the slow organisation of wheelchairs.*

Past Montreux terraces stepped to shingle
as the railway wandered beside the lake.

Alone he watched mist engulf the far shore,
saw hipped-gable houses, neat balconies,

the kempt and regular fields, unfenced lines
of winter vineyards matrixing the land.

Thin-boned elms wore their promise of
    catkins,
expectant of spring and praising the sky.

Everywhere was tidy, respectable.
Rooks, black as undertakers, pecked in rows.

They could've landed closer to the clinic
but she longed to pass the lake once more.

Years ago she'd swum there every morning,
a foreign exchange student in Lausanne.

Last week as they'd left Lac Leman behind
she'd said it was her favourite time of year

"...you can really feel the winter passing".

SCARE

At first he didn't hear the tractor's growl
for the larks. The sky was a well of blue
and the high stems of elephant grass
rattled over him, tall as playground bullies.
The dog was there somewhere chasing its nose
while he wandered shouting through the
    wicker.

The sun's position should've been a guide
but the acreage was vast and he was mazed -
till the wind carried down the tractor's sound
(a combine, harvesting the yellow canes?)
and he started to run, zigzagging through
the dusty stalks like a hounded rabbit.

Still the machine came, its silver threshers
relentlessly chopping, hunting him down...
He burst from the cackling crop exhausted
and there was the dog, the lane and the trees;
the faraway sea - and way over the fields
a lonely tractor slanting the green turf.

Sunlight stripes us through the wavering stalks
as we lie breathless and high, listening
to the frantic insistence of skylarks,
feeling our hearts recover, pulses slow,
numb to all time but this one moment,
wild within the elephant grass raffia,
its thin shadow grid moving across us,
so if we half close our eyes we flicker
like the final frames of an old film show
about jailbreak runaways who outwit
the hounds and strip off in a southern field,
shedding more arrows than eager Cupid,
only to find their malnourished bodies
tattooed with a sweet and biblical crime.

I Dreamed of a River

A painted river moves through my dreams.
Some mornings I wake gasping,
beached on the shore of an imagined life.

I went to see a hokum diviner,
described the water, its turbulence
battering my heart, filling my lungs.

She asked the colour of the scene:
egret at first light, red deer at dusk.
What words pooled upon my pillow?

I told her I saw the river's gillie
moving slowly through whispering flies
miles from the lonely water meadows.

She asked if the river was unhappy?
I couldn't say. How could I know a river?
All I knew is I was pulled to its flow,

to the small shy fish, the slip of pebbles
glinting under alder boughs,
pond skaters testing the river's rind,

and the drenched velvet depths
folded and dark as Ophelia's cape
billowing in the gravel and the cress.

Close stepped alleys sweat together,
entwine and climb this cliff face town.

They are
        - my sleeping lover's leg
           hooked softly over my thigh,
           her sirocco breath on my neck;

        - warm April sun filtering down
           a false atlas of cracked plaster;
           dark as a damp archway;

        - revelatory, bursting
           into a bright piazza,
           the splash of creamy sunlight.

We roll apart and trail our own
strange shuttered alleys till morning.

As midnight tolled its long count
our host Stefano tumbled down
into the oleander plants
around the border of the lawn.

Distant valley dogs were barking
as we pulled him from the fiori,
laughing and unspectacled.
We offered our *grazie mille*

then left along separate paths,
diverging from the lantern light
into the spark-peppered darkness
of a new-moon summer night.

Feeling for the crumbled asphalt
with the soles of wandering shoes,
I recalled Maria's warning
about fierce cinghiali sows.

At an unremembered bend,
which may have curled its way to home
or the dereliction of a ditch,
a chariot of fireflies came

to carry me high and waving
like a flag of *well, whatever*
over olives, figs and walnuts,
then down from the wild Maiella

to the tattered edge of town
where leathery lucciole
wait for secret charioteers;
the depot where Giuseppe

works early morning shifts
before tending to his nursery
of aubergines and peppers;
the broken-windowed factories

empty by the autostrada;
the seaside conurbation
sleeping for a sunny day;
then back, over corrugations

of coppi, to set me down swirly
at my door. How many it took
to fly a drunk I can't be sure
they disappeared before I looked

but this I know my clothes were torn
my shoes were in a dreadful state
- you let the fireflies light you home
and this'll be the price you pay.

*'To take fireflies for lanterns' is an Italian expression
meaning 'to get the wrong end of the stick'.
Lucciole means fireflies but is also Italian slang
for prostitutes.*

JUMP

Under the cafe's awning
you watch the sky haemorrhage.

Storms die in their own time,
maybe minutes, sometimes days.

Unable to decipher the sky
or press the cloud's pulse,

you only know soon you must go,
coatless, on to the bloodied road.

For now though you wait,
caffeinated, sprung, late.

The smell of breakfast, the soft hubbub,
the clinking waitress, are all behind you.

A woman emerges, waits too.
She's in a coat the colour of scrubs.

Are you alright? she asks.
You stare out into the deluge,

the glazed river-road, the vulgar torrent,
the beating heart of thunder.

Come back inside... she smiles,
taking your hand, afraid you will jump.

That was the year my apparitions came,
white ember phantoms, arising each dawn
to trail through ash groves and wild country
    lanes.

Ghosts in the wheat field were shaking the
    grain
and children's voices called over bright lawns.
That was the year my apparitions came.

High in the elm trees the rooks cawed their
    claim.
The sweat of the river lay in long shrouds,
dimpsy down ash groves and wild country
    lanes.

Bone-leaves tumbled to earth and autumn rain
rattled the rusty sheds housing the cows.
That was the year my apparitions came.

Something was taken I won't have again.
The wind shook the wands in the hazel copse,
worried the ash trees down wild country lanes.

Death plays Hangman, just a child at its game,
completing the scaffold, drawing the corpse.
That was the year my apparitions came,
blowing the ashes down wild country lanes.

THE GREEN WAYS

Old track-ways still score this land.
Thin trails crossing hilly pasture
from one hedge break to another.
Paths trodden through nettle-patches;
stink lines laid by stoat and vixen.
The badger-barged under-brush.

Routes of rain and least resistance
running the ridge above the fall,
terraced by frost and slippage
where our slumbering planet
pulled its soiled blankets,
shaking down bedbugs and mud.

Before the map and compass,
before the scratching of lines in dust,
before partition and hedgerow -
even before instinct and pointing,
we wandered these animal ways
guided by the nervousness of deer.

We lay down in hares' depressions
the *forms* where leverets once laid.
We cut through to overhung rivers,
the bright roads of brown trout,
blackberry bushes and the low
sunny places where strawberries grew.

Licking honeycomb and listening
we sheltered in dark holly-houses.
Bees were impossible at first
but all habits become clear in time
to the patient watcher, the hive hunter,
the egg finder, the salmon snagger.

It was settling that changed things.
Finding a hill-fort to call your own.
Possession - the mine and yours of it -
needs demarcation, diagram,
then new trades of draughtsman,
hedge-layer, henchman, lawyer.

I watch the birds arrive in spring.
The martins come back every year
navigating over sea by air braille.
No shared map, no rights of way,
just feeling the face of places.
A river mouth; a head of hornbeams.

And here in this Devon garden
itinerant rabbits come and go
between next doors' cabbages and mine
ignorant of deeds and boundaries
eating where they will, leaving their tithe
of worthless currency behind.

The Tree's Contract

To wear your lungs on the outside.
To stretch up many-elbowed arms,
holding those lungs high
where the circulating air
might best refresh their alveoli.

To resist with crinkle-armoured trunk
the beetle's bite, the bleeding canker,
leaf miner moth and wild hive.
To wear the tattooed hearts and arrows
of teenage lovers' penknives.

To give rent-free lofts to nesting birds
and not count the progeny launched
from the scaffold of your limbs
except by equation -
the x times y of your annular rings.

To wave goodbye to summer
wearing gloves of red and yellow.
To thrust and spur by Fibonacci.
To offer catkins, cones and conkers.
To parse the winter sky through filigree.

To speak your words as a seismic pulse.
To bud and bluster, turn and fall.
To give your heart to a sideboard and chairs.
And when it's time: to burn and crackle
- Ash to ashes, to smoke, winnowing in air.

RAW

I log the fallen chestnut
This bright, frank morning.
The rackety saw,
my soft hands,
unaccustomed, raw.

So damn cold...
The grass crunches
and crystals shine all
along the crumbling
red brick garden wall.

My throat hacks twice,
my breath is caught
escaping and suspended,
above my arm, the saw
and the chestnut trunk, upended.

I want to stop this now
but greater want the pain.
The frozen ground,
the low slung sun,
the saw's coarse sound.

Such physicality
the heat and cold:
life's elemental law.
Beyond our pink rooms
hard earth awaits us, raw.

EXTINCTION EASTER
EASTER 2019

After this 'Hottest Easter Monday'
I sit in my garden at night
hearing the roar of a motorbike
revving through the curves
way over on the coast road.
The noise shouldn't carry this far
but tonight it stretches through the dry hills
drawn by the density of the air.
Rain is coming soon, I can feel it
in my nose; my ears; weighing on my skin.
The grass will suddenly remember,
the trees sit up and pay attention.

But now I'm sitting with a beer
and a chapbook of poems
sent to me by Stella in France.
Fine as they are I can't concentrate.
My shirt smells of old sweat,
the beer tastes like tin and her words
melt and run before my stale eyes.
Over the distant glow of town
a muffled helicopter churns
the gathering clouds like a milk whisk.
Thunder will burst this bubble tomorrow;
temperatures will fall to where they should be.

Then we can all moan again about April rain
and forget the *right-fucking-now* of climate
    change.

Heat

The field maples have laid their small palms
    down,
still green, as if autumn arrived early
too flustered and hot for a change of gown.

On a midweek lunch break walking through
    town
an obese man faints queuing for ice cream.
Office boys and shop girls are all beach-brown.

Our planet has heated by one degree.
The reporter drones on, nobody screams.
These are the days before catastrophe.

Late Friday evening we switch off tv,
drive down to the beach for a midnight swim,
the water skillet-flat, jellyfish free.

Far out on the endless pan tiny lights
slip off into blackness over the rim
lured by a siren call of satellites.

We make a fire with the refuse to hand
(dried flotsam, white sickly bones of the sea),
then stargaze on beds of plastic and sand.

See? White bugles of bindweed covering
the back wheels and PTO. Ferguson,
late forties before the Massey merger.

And this one shows foxgloves, two metres high
making short work of a common Fordson.
Bees love them. Hard to tell what year it is.

Here's a rarity: a Caterpillar!
Think of the sheer weight of metal in that...
See how it's bogged down in stinging nettles?

This one's a Kubota - not too many
made it over here. Japanese Knotweed
growing right up into the frame and seat.

I love the patina of perished tyres
dulled grey by sunlight and rain, the silence
of a seized block in an abandoned yard.

I'm hoping for a good Lamborghini
(before they started with frivolous cars)
rusting red in a patch of zucchini.

Rewilding Stonelands Farm

See this:
a red flatbed marooned in slurry,
a perished tyre up on top
of a rusted Peugeot raised on blocks,
a green trailer laden with sodden logs.
Last night's storm has passed
and everything steams
as if the world is being poached.
A squirrel shuffles hazels,
clanging the galvanised tin
of a purposeless shed.
At the island end
of a waterlogged paddock
five black heifers wait
for nothing they can name.
Mystery machinery
corrodes against stone,
caught by surprise
when the iron plague came.
On a yellow skip throne
a one horned quad bike
rules this junk and rubble kingdom.
Behind a high fence,
something happened
The Planners wouldn't like.
A snapped sign says:
    Private Kee

Nothing moves. I wait
and nothing moves again.
The Earth is readying itself
to accept a death, the slow
disassembly of molecules.
See this: empty pubs, silent schools.

INHERITANCE

The roof is leaking.
Fred will mend it
with a storm-flung slate
relinquished by the barn.
Inside the kettle's creaking
on the stove near simple
Aunt Leticia keeping warm.

Margarine, linoleum and oil
seep from the wallpaper like fog.
Two tomcats sizzle by the boiler,
troubled dreams disturb an unloved dog.

The rain sings on the iron roof
above the animal shed.
It runs between the crinkles,
down the gutter to the trough.
The matted cattle within,
restless in their excrement,
stamp and steam and snort and cough.

Quiet in the hay barn,
warm enough out of the wind,
John hangs lifeless from the rafters,
waiting, turning, for Fred to find.

BADGERS

My house retreats into the warm June night.
A hi-viz spangle of scattered glow worms
decorates the verge and soft-lowing cows
murmur in the dew-mist shrouding the fields.

Up the lane Alan is watching a film.
I can hear American characters
shooting bad fellows like there's no sequel.
The travesties float from open windows.

He is unaware that two big badgers
are stripe-snouting through his dahlia bed
and marking out his lawn. They'll be searching
for bodies under the patio next.

When wolves move out to hunt the hare
and stars burn coldly through the spheres,
dark forests fill with whispered prayer
where snow falls thick and drifts are sheer
and those that can stay in their lair
for night is full of hungered fear;
old owls heed all who hunker there:
the stag horn beetle, stealthy deer,
scraggy vixen and hulking bear,
yet always hold their knowledge near:
Who? Who?
            the only words they'll share;
Who? Who?
            their questions ringing clear -
through bronze-hung beeches, freezing air
- are winter bells no man will hear.

RAKINEWIS – THE CAPESTRANO WARRIOR

For the ruination of Palmyra and after Shelley

His shroud was campion in May;
a king's cape of crocus in November.
Curled olive roots held him in the afterlife
like the fingers of forgotten gods.
For two and a half millennia
blinking skies cycled over him -
until a contadino's plough tipped his hat
and he was exhumed for wonder.

When we first met he was standing
bright and alone in a cold mausoleum,
arms across his sword and belly
as if shivering - plucked from his bed -
his shadow cast upon cream walls.

> *I'm not of this place, this cave*
> *is not my necropolis - free me,*
> *take me back to Picenum,*
> *lay me under the stony soil*
> *so I may hear again the soft*
> *spiking of rain on the grass,*
> *feel the bulbs questing in spring,*
> *hear my woodpeckers calling.*

At dawn we drove in a hired Mercedes,
him gazing out at the new world
laid like a loose flag on the Abruzzi hills.
I recounted the Hellenic period,
the Romans, the Social Wars, the Empire,
Christ and the Popes, the Internecine Wars,
the Twentieth Century. It took a while.

Could I have been king of all this - 'King of Kings'?

From the old stone town of Capestrano
we looked to the ruins of Rocca Calascio,
circled by jackdaws and hooded crows,
a thousand years weather beaten
- and all of it startling and new to him.
Below us a tractor scratched the soil
beside a black hectare of solar panels.

> *See how the Greeks left, Rome fell?*
> *Nothing has remained unchallenged*
> *for as long as I ruled my dark grave,*
> *humming quietly to the beat of the sun,*
> *the business of earth worms.*
> *Where am I safest? Below the loyal soil*
> *rolling with the terremoti,*
> *or standing bold in lime light*
> *exposed to the motives of terror,*
> *the certainty of political change:*
> *invaders with their own gods,*
> *who may not care for an old stone king?*

But both of us knew everything had changed.
His necropolis scattered, his sleep broken.
We drove in silence to the Campo Imperatore
where the lone and level plain stretched
    far away
before turning back to the foothills.
I promised to bring him campion in May
and a regal fist of crocuses in November.

Ah, and when you're gone, who'll bring me
flowers then?

All afternoon the old grey dog
curled in a depression of his own shape
under a lattice of palm fronds.

Through a break in the rocks
spent waves ricocheted
over coral, cowry, crab-shell.

Farther along at the beach bar
people were packing away towels,
scooping up snorkels and masks.

Settled under tables other strays
lay in the soft-clinking shade
waiting for scraps of kindness.

The grey dog was removed from all that.
He'd taken himself off to lie down, let go.
To collapse into singularity.

When I was twelve or so
our old Dalmatian took sick,
slouched off into the fields.

Dogs do that when they know things are bad,
my father said
they want to be alone, let nature take its course.

I searched for Sam all afternoon,
found him shivering and guilty-faced
in the long grass of a fallow field.

I carried his surrendered weight
half a mile home and for a while
the vet staved off death.

All dogs must die somewhere.
It could be good out of the breeze,
shaded by broad banana leaves.

Early next day I followed the clay path down
from the tuk-tuk turn, past the hut
where women in saris sold coconuts,

past the unrendered houses where small,
shirtless kids were already out in their yards
shouting *hello!* to passing strangers.

I looked for the dog.
He'll be gone, of course.
He'll have picked himself up,

shaken off the sand,
wandered away to seek
another day's salvation.

Or maybe he will have quietly died,
borne east into the morning
on a yellow Indian Ocean

with the green turtles,
the blue whales and all the gaudy
whale-watching boats?

Except there he was,
dead as any old grey dog,
any old grey dog on a waking beach,

a banana leaf across his flat haunches,
and a butchery of land crabs
trickling toward him over the sand.

We took a boat out for Golden Mahseer,
fishing the greedy Ganges, casting flies
across its race as logs and rags spun by.
It seemed a futile hunt until - what luck! -
a charred body neared, fallen from a pyre,
preyed upon by a shoal of roiling fish.

As this hellish vision drifted closer
my angling friend reeled in his lure and line,
remade his tackle with a pink 'flesh fly'
then cast into the froth around the corpse.
I looked away. On the bank women washed,
above the trees a little minaret
shone through the smog framed sun. What can
    be said?
We fished for fish which fed upon the dead.

Fishing with Olivia

After the vernal equinox
the wind shook the trees awake.
Suddenly the woods were clothed.

We rose with songbirds and flew to the hills
and a stream in spate from moorland thunder.
Winter-thin fish flickered in spinning pools -
listless but hungry for a Gold-Head Nymph.

I hooked a brook trout, my hands trembling.
Soon I'll struggle to tie a fly.
I'm on the dark side of my equinox
but happy hearing you chatter,
budding towards your perfect days of June.

That night the March wind forced a roundelay
from the choir of trees: *Springeth the wud nu!*
and I lay like an old fish recalling
all the water flowed through me and away,

every drop stealing a scale,
fining me to my essence
and into the wild singing trees.

*'Springeth the wud nu' is taken from
'Sumer is icumen in' a C.12 round in the
medieval Wessex dialect.*

The Disappearing Places

Adrift in the déjà vu of sleep,
I climb a gate taller than me
to follow sheep-trails
down Farmer Strang's
tussocky pastures
to the fir tree spinney.

Nettle-banked marl pits
hold a glory of perch,
fierce-finned and dark-barred.
Out of olive depths
I pull a mud-lipped tench
small-eyed and gasping.

A winding grass snake
tows a sine wave of itself
over the pond's limp face
and I catch it in the reeds,
holding it by its yellow collar
till it stinks itself, feigning death.

Why does the spinney pull me back?

So much skin I've sloughed
since I caught that secret tench,
held high that tangle of snake
and walked with a knife,
a rod, and my own name
for all the disappearing places.

The Slender Child

She weighed barely more
than her satchel of crayons
as the paramedics scooped
up her snapped body.

So slight, the little girl
was nearly translucent,
thin as the five o'clock light
bouncing off broken glass.

The driver sat on the verge,
his phone lying in the grass,
thrown like a hot stone.
Facebook held its breath.

The October afternoon
was wandering away,
its pale sky itching with a
hashtag of radio waves.

The police took names,
measurements, photos, time.
Diversions were arranged.
The light slowly degraded

like a soft pencil line
pulled across a register.

When he said goodbye
near the holiday flats
and the wind flipped away
her Kiss-Me-Quick hat
and he laughed that *No!*
It hadn't been 'crap'!
- he couldn't tell then
that if he had snapped
her slim waist in two
his name was inked there
running all the way through.

Stabbing orange beaks into kelp and wrack
they collect dark weed to cover a child
lying naked where the tide licks the land.

The baby is dead but the birds can't tell,
compelled by a biblical instinct
to hide her from some unseen pursuer.

No one knows the mother's name, how she
        came,
why she strapped such a cross of pain to
        herself,
leaving her baby on a cockling sack.

The small corpse, layered with weed, might be
a washed up jellyfish, a salt bleached stump.
The birds scatter to sand spars and rocks.

Long ago they concealed a different child,
cowering under a coat of seaweed
and the count of time itself was altered.

Black flags emblazoned with white crosses
tip in the cold breeze. The Mussel Pickers,
the Sea Pies, whine like a winded klaxon.

*There is an old Celtic legend that the child Christ visited the
Western Isles. While there he was pursued by enemies and hid on a
beach where oystercatchers assisted him by covering him with
weed. In 2002 a new born baby was found dead on the estuary
beach at Archbrook, near Shaldon in Devon.
No parent was ever located.*

Baited hooks at both ends, cruelty was laid
along the sea wall. Two gulls, slaves to faith,
lunged, swallowed, rose up - so snagging the
    barbs
in their gullets. The six foot line went taut -

and round they whirled, enraged adversaries,
wrenching their throats; over the sea and back,
a self propelled, feathered boleadoras
spinning down to crash on the promenade.

The yobs legged it, blurting profanities.
Two women, still as lecterns, hands on mouths
had no idea what to do, who to call.
A tattooed girl took photos with her phone.

Beyond the disgust there's recognition:
this is the way God works in everything.

THE BIRD SCARER

He dug into the wormy earth and raised
a makeshift crucifix of two-by-four.

Over torn denim work clothes stuffed with hay
he pulled an orange dress to catch the wind.

Her head: a feed sack filled with muddy straw
crowned by a long discarded wedding hat.

Spreading his arms wide he tipped his head
    back,
closed his eyes and faced off the gaping sky.

In the moment the two of them hung there
a multitude of earthworms moved the soil,

the corn grew high as a millipede's leg
and the trees crackled with ravenous birds.

Then a banger went off, rooks clattered up,
and he left her to flutter in her maize.

GREEN MAN IN ROCOMBE

I saw a Green Man fleetingly,
standing close by the farm-shop's barn.
The height of a tall hawthorn tree
and dappled in the rising sun.
For that bird-song moment he stopped
(as early morning vapours cleared
to tangle round the bramble tops),
looked my way then disappeared.

Not wistful at the summer's cease
the gentle closing of the year,
but smiling in a hat of leaves,
garlanded with rose-hip and sloe,
he vanished like a startled deer
or ermine on new winter snow.

After the asteroid struck the moon
the sky was speckled with falling stars.
For weeks we puzzled on frosty lawns
tilting backwards to gaze at the wound.
Christians climbed hills singing for rapture.
The Dow and Footsie fell.

Now the moon smiles with a missing tooth:
a bruised and pock-marked fairground barker.
Fishermen complain the tides are failing,
the sea is torpid, the fish have no fight.
On the littered beach doubtful scientists
measure the rise and fall.

I'm sleepless at five and riddled with thought:
a motor and flywheel, a broken belt?
Into the dark kitchen most of the moon
shines over the roof of my neighbour's farm.
Naked and thirsty I peel tangerines,
feel them squirt on my skin.

A light comes on by the milking parlour,
the laden cows start clanking their stalls,
lunatic bovines, they low for the pull.
I eat the moon, segment by segment,
leaving the peel in a silver dish,
a votive for its hurt.

THE HUM

Six in the morning early December
the night sky still pitch. I'm too cold to look
upward at the universal glitter
and I've a long expected meeting booked.

Yet by the front door I pause, key in hand.
I can hear The Hum. Faint, low and constant
in the quiet of the unbroken dawn.
Its direction: everywhere - but distant.

A diesel warming up? Or staying warm
the way idling engines run all night
on northern driveways gripped by permafrost?
High echoes from a transatlantic flight?

Perhaps a strange insomniac farmer
doing unfathomable tractor chores
hours before the first squeak of pallid light.
No. Not these but something else. Something
    more...

A billion refrigerators purring;
the Earth stiffly grinding on its axis;
quiet pulsations in the veins of mice;
thin fluid seeping through dormant insects.

The soft rhythm of our hearts, yours and mine.
You asleep and me preparing for - what?
Driving west to resilient darkness
and a dawn of hospital lights, I watch
the sky grow pink in my rear view mirror.

Out of the box comes a crumpled scrapbook
with flamingos snipped from World of Wonder
and a class project with paintings by kids
whose crayoned names conjure few faces.
And this: a purple silk sports day ribbon,
a triumphal laureate - a beauty
the colour of a dead-leg bruise.
Most likely for sack race or egg and spoon.

I was an uncoordinated child:
throw a ball to me and my weedy arms -
useless and white as lilies in the wind -
would be up and waving, a squint
contorting my desperate face
as I prepared for a hit in the teeth
two seconds after it had passed.

So this small ribbon, almost certainly
a third place despite its regal shade,
was special to the ten-year-old me,
a validation, a dopamine high
for a kid picked last from playground lineups
by football captains, those pre-teen marvels
of athleticism whom I now know
were simply born early in the school year.

Shot-silk declaring I could keep an egg
balanced on a wooden spoon while jogging
over new-mown grass and worm casts,
a feat I'd fail at now since this shaking
came upon me unreasonably early
and without levodopa I can't take tea
unspilled from the kitchen to the lounge.

But perhaps it was the three legged race?
Maybe I was hobbled and tethered
to another, a stronger person
who pulled me to the finishing tape?
I place the stuff back in the box -
not ready to burn it quite yet -
as my wife, steady handed as always,
crosses the line with two mugs of tea.

We're almost at the nadir,
the point where day and night
get as far as they can
in their struggle to change place.
It was nearly eight in the morning
and black as a stack of tyres.
The A&E department was quiet,
shift workers with cracked limbs,
old men whose hearts had been
clutched at by the greedy night.
The guy on the plastic chair
next to me had only one eye
which flicked around like a pinball
as he made this pronouncement.
Mind you, it's always half light for me...
he half smiled. *So what you in for?*
People are never supposed to ask that.
Our personal hurts are a box of delights
shared only with receptionists and medics.
Fear of the dark I replied *like everyone else.*

The China Cupboard

I'm opening the cupboard
searching for a soup bowl,
cake plate, pestle, mortar,
that blue Chinese rice dish,
taking things out putting them back
but I can't find whatever it is
and start hurling stuff
on the quarry tiled floor,
so I should apologise -
this shatter of crockery
must've waken you though I know
it's all in my head, it just feels
as if you should hear it,
but then you open your eyes,
say you've been awake for ages,
the birds or the dog or me turning,
the noise of me breathing and I think
Noise..? you don't know the half of it -
have you seen the kitchen floor?
so I take several deep breaths
try to listen to the garden birds,
feel the wide Wedgwood sky
passing in slow motion,
calm myself and in so doing I hear
a catastrophe of cut glass and crystal
falling in the cabinet of fine bone
and mystery between your ears.

THE RIVER AND THE WIND

The river ran fast behind the houses
from where, on a daytime TV morning,
she gazed blankly out past shirts and blouses
hung in suburban breeze slowly drying

and wondered what their kids were doing now.
She didn't watch the river and the wind
but clicked the kettle on to make a brew,
took milk from the fridge, teabags from the tin,

then, while waiting on the kettle's clamour,
slipped her cold hands inside her bra and
    squeezed
her breasts too hard - like a clumsy doctor.
She knew one day she'd find signs of disease.

A pea sized lump? A malignant tumour?
In the end what else was there to wait for?

Sleep Walking

i.m. Judy Woodward

You were sleeping when the syringe drivers
    came -
you woke to apparatus by your bed.
In the kitchen the solemn doctor said
I can't tell, no two patients are the same
but it won't be long now, we're talking days.
We hugged each other then cried some more,
made tea, took turns in popping to the store,
each trip outside a respite in its way.

I recall a ringing phone but not who spoke.
You mostly slept, just drifting in and out,
and though one of us was there if you awoke
looking back I think we slept-walked with you,
step-by-step until that place beyond all doubt
where you released our hands to slip on
    through.

CARPE DIEM

i.m. Mervyn Woodward

'…the priest and the doctor
in their long coats
running over the fields'.
('Days' Philip Larkin)

I stopped near the house
of my dead parents,
down a thin lane
pinned by the wind
to vegetable fields,
where unwalked footpaths,
like a map of memory loss,
searched for settlements
long ploughed over.

They retired to Devon
for their last years together,
filling the bird-feeder,
bending to the garden,
stretching laundry
across the wind.

It was a spring weekend,
days whistle-brisk
and bright as this one,
rain always around
the corner of the sky,
when we went to clear
out their cottage,
sorting, remembering,
facing their pasts,
and closer, our own.

Now, at the five bar gate
where my father leaned
to watch his dog run itself
across tumbled furrows,
I wonder what he used
to think about. Was it
that I didn't call enough?
My mother would always say
I should call him more
but looking back it was
probably her I should've rung.

I could talk to you
about impermanence
but it'd be nothing
you don't already know.
For God's sake:
seize the day and shake it!
Shake it upside down
till all its bright coins
fall around your feet.
Gather them and buy
a slow-ticking watch,
a suit of conversation,
a hat of laughter,
wear them every day
until you hear those
dark-clothed felons
running over the fields
so sure of their
Gladstone and their bible.

MAY THE FIFTH, 2020
(THERE IS NO MELANCHOLY WITHOUT RAIN)

There is no melancholy without rain.
Edna's rain *full of ghosts that tap and sigh*,
Edward's *wild midnight rain* blessing the dead
Hardy's *raindrop ploughing down a carved name* -
sadness is only amplified by rain.
Perhaps that's why this April, hot and dry,
we just nested, watched light TV instead
of switching on the dreadful news again.

On May the fifth the sunny weather broke.
It rained from after midnight all the way
till after lunch. I thought of the lives changed
and in me a deeper sympathy woke
for the sorrow of strangers - those who lay
in afternoon bedrooms locked down with rain.

SONNET ON AN OLD SCARF OF MY MOTHER'S

Are you still here in fine atomic form?
Some tiny particle embedded yet
within the weave, indelible - a germ
time won't allow the fabric to forget?
Would forensic scientists with lab coats,
chemicals and electron microscopes
confirm that yes indeed, your hand brushed
    here
and through this fibrous mesh you once
    exhaled,
your soft breath passing like a captive's tears
evaporating from a woollen gaol?
Funny then I choose this rag to bind my face -
not to inhale some dissipated trace
of your perfume - (what was it that you wore..?)
but to help the vulnerable stay secure.

SUMMER SOLSTICE 2020

These are the sharp nights
known to medieval cities
when the watchman's pay

was light in his pocket
and cock-crow barrow men
came yawning their shouts.

Hasn't our task always been
the calibration of night,
the numbering of darkness?

In rock-temple silence
the Gods and Men try
long distance calling

while out on the timeless hills
mid-summer deer move
viral through the ash.

Seven moth and nightjar hours
to wheedle reconciliation
certain the night will lengthen

soft as sun on standing stones.
Still, I wonder: might dying young
be better than dying alone?

Vincent couldn't sit still.
While I was fiddling with my phone
he was looking round at the view,
the girls, the Adriatic colours.

When we went for a swim
he kept his straw hat on.
I waddled on hard pebbles,
stubbed my toe; he smiled.

He asked if we could visit Fazio's
on the way back. I agreed.
I knew he'd order Sambuca
then wince at its sweetness.

I think he liked the green hills,
the fortified villages,
vineyards and farmsteads,
ancient and scatter-down.

We were rubbing along okay,
I figured he'd stick around
but we drove to the coast today
and while I swam he vanished.

Maybe he was troubled
by the lack of sunflowers;
perhaps just pining for France?
He wasn't much of a talker.

I stopped at Fazio's bar
and drank a cold Peroni,
under a blue umbrella
my back to the warm wall.

The persimmon sun sank down
and all his whirling stars came slowly
out and I thought of Vincent
rolling with the pebbles in the sea.

Imagine a church stripped. Naked.
The gaudy regalia removed:
the carved saints, oiled madonnas,
overbearing blood and nails.
Unaccommodating oak pews
that serve to punish and remind
the sad and fatally resigned.
The eagle lecterns, the stupid board
flipped over like a cricket score
advising the number of the psalm.
The useless tapestry hassocks
that cause arthritic knees more harm.
All of it - the gross carapace,
the instrument of control - erased.

Then accept this space: a retreat
from the sun, the rain, the blabber.
White stone walls a thousand years hewn.
Outside, by steepled cypresses,
a hoopoe hops, while kids clutch towels
heading for the purge of the stream.
If you're inclined to bend and pray
you couldn't find a calmer place.
Rest your hands here and contemplate
the construct of your history,
like a mason remembering
the walls he built when he was young,
hurrying and keen, knowing now
how he could have laid them better.

Bong!
The tower
is hollow,
you know.
No substance -
just a sham
of winding steps,
slitty windows
and a cool
down draught
on summer days.
The view from
the cupola
is fine they say
but I can't
overlook
the fragility
of the
thin air
beneath me,
and the
worry of an
architect
wearing
the Doge's
new clothes.

ABOUT THE AUTHOR

Although a New Yorker by birth, Marc Woodward has been a lifelong resident of rural England. His writing reflects his surroundings in the remote West Country, often with a dark undercurrent — and a degree of wry humour.

He has been widely published in journals, anthologies and online.

He was writer-in-residence at The Wellstone Center in Santa Cruz, California, in 2018, shortlisted for the 2018 Bridport Prize, commended for the 2020 Acumen Poetry Prize and the 2020 Aesthetica Creative Writing Award.

In addition to writing, he is also an accomplished musician who has recorded, performed, and taught internationally.

"Beautifully crafted poems...that sing in the dark of darkness."
Canto Magazine

ABOUT THE PRESS

Sea Crow Press is named for a flock of five talkative crows you can find anywhere on the beach between Scudder Lane and Bone Hill Road in Barnstable Village on Cape Cod.

According to Norse legend, one-eyed Odin sent two crows out into the world so they could return and tell him its stories. If you sit and listen to the sea crows in Barnstable as they fly and roost and chatter, it's an easy legend to believe.

Sea Crow Press is committed to amplifying voices that might otherwise go unheard with a focus on positive change and great storytelling. Founded in 2020, the growing press is home to an eclectic collection of creative nonfiction, fiction, and poetry. At Sea Crow Press we believe the small press plays an essential part in contemporary arts by amplifying its voices. Sea Crow Press is committed to building an accessible community of writers and dedicated to telling stories that matter.

Lightning Source UK Ltd.
Milton Keynes UK
UKHW041152271122
412909UK00005B/125

9 798985 008005